THE KLUTZ BOOK OF MAGIC

by John Cassidy
and Michael "Magic Mike" Stroud

illustrated by
H.B. Lewis
and Sara Boore

KLUTZ®

TABLE OF CONTENTS

Magic

Why You Are Reading This Book   4

Your First Trick   5

How to Do Magic   7

The Magician's Blood Oath   8

May I Cut Off Your Pinky?   10

Young Clips in Love   12

The Broom and Egg Whap   14

Thread the Needle   16

A Pocketful of Fraud   18

The French Drop   20

Where's the Rub?   24

Lindbergh's Hankie   26

The Best Trick in this Book   28

The Vanishing Salt Shaker   30

Weird Gravity Coins   33

Siamese Twin Ropes   36

Rope Handcuffs   40

Gypsy Switch   42

The Magic Egg   46

Tricks

The Great American Nasal Band   48

Psychic Silverware   50

Thumbs Up Ring Release   52

Spinning Ring Release   54

Ring Flip   56

The Liko Pang Penetration   58

The Rubber Band Impossibility   62

Nutty String   63

The Ring Slide   66

Ring Zing   69

Cut and Restored Rope   72

The Center Tear   76

The Flip and Flop Force   78

Spook Writing   80

The Fruit Card Trick   83

Thumb Tip Pointers   86

The Vanishing Scarf   88

Silken Dollar   90

Cut and Restored Ribbon   94

Why
You Are Reading
This Book

Because, like most people, you've never read anybody's mind, made a scarf emerge from a dollar bill, or reincarnated a dead playing card inside an orange.

You've never beamed a quarter into a perfectly sealed drinking glass, or turned a volunteer's dollar bill into thin air, right before his horrified eyes. You've never restored a cut-up length of rope into a single piece again, or rolled up your sleeves and vanished a coin mere inches from your audience's nose. You've never, let's face it, been truly amazing.

The performance of magic is arguably the most ancient of all human arts, with a pedigree that stretches back to the caves, if not the trees (the old "Banana Vanish"). Magic is performance, acting, the telling of tall physical tales. A magician trains to make every word and motion lead his trusting, innocent audience into a completely ridiculous, completely inescapable trap. What could be more human?

Your First TRICK

You're probably not aware of this medical fact, but as your eyes scan these words, a certain percentage of the mental energy necessary for reading leaks out from under your "cranial cap" and escapes. It's not a large percentage, but this energy (in the form of Beta-waves) radiates outward in all directions equally. Most of the waves, of course, are lost to the void of outer space, but a few of them are able to bounce off the ionosphere. When they get back to earth, the great majority of the Beta-waves are absorbed harmlessly by inert materials (plywood, Naugahyde and so forth), but a tiny percentage of them are capable of stimulating the "hyposensitive synaptic glands" of certain unique individuals. Scientists refer to this whole phenomenon — which has just recently been discovered — as "intercranial communication." You or I would call it "mind reading." Unfortunately, the "synaptic gland" is a recessive characteristic — found in only a tiny percentage of the population. And "hyposensitive" synaptic glands are even rarer. Leading scientists estimate that there are only nine people in the world with properly functioning hyposensitive synaptic glands. Which makes it all the more amazing when you realize that the author of these lines is one of them. That's right. This very instant, as you read these words, I am reading minds, yours in particular. Don't be frightened or alarmed, and don't try to resist. It's useless. The entire process is beyond conscious control. Perhaps you're dubious. Some people are. Fortunately, I can prove my claim beyond any possible doubt. I'll close my eyes for a second in order to focus… "Just a moment…

There!!! I Have It! You're Thinking That I Can't Read MINDS!"

5

That was my first magic trick.

I learned it in grammar school many years ago and I have never tired of it. Although I am told others do. Here are a few others in the same vein (except better).

Pick a number:
1 2
3
4 Why 3?

Sequel #1: Write the numbers "1… 2… 3… 4" on a piece of paper. Hold it up and ask a volunteer to silently pick one. After a moment's concentration, turn the paper around where you've written the words "Why 3?" You'll be right about half the time (which ain't bad).

Sequel #2: Secretly, write "35" on your palm. Don't let your volunteer see anything and then ask them to "…pick a number. Silently. *Between 1 and 50.*"

Give them a moment, then change the rules: "But it has to be two digits. Both odd. **DON'T TELL ME!** But hurry up. This is just the first step. There's more."

When they tell you they've got it, stare at the ceiling for a while, close your eyes, foam at the mouth… whatever looks like you're concentrating. Finally… *finally*… announce "Your number is… 37!!"

One of three things will happen:

1. You'll be right, they picked "37" (which happens about half the time, amazingly).

2. But say you're wrong. The number was "35" they tell you (next most common choice). Say "I don't believe you!"

Then press your palm to their forehead, like you were checking for a fever. Pull it away, look at your palm, show them it's "35" and apologize: "Sorry, I guess you *were* telling the truth…"

3. None of the above. They picked some weird number.

No problem. Just explain that a very few people have such tiny brains ("you know, like those dinosaurs") that they send out extremely low wattage that's basically impossible to read. ("But the good news, you're a rare one!")

This may be a lame trick, but it demonstrates a classic magician's ploy which I will italicize because it is so important:

When you're using a volunteer, always have Plan B in mind, in case they take a left turn when you're looking for a right.

HOW TO DO MAGIC

Actually, that's a trick headline. Magic is not done, it's performed! Like any performance art, it withers away to nothing if it's not presented in the grand style. Moving your feet around is not dancing, reading the lyrics is not singing, and pulling a rabbit out of a hat is not magic. There's a little more to it than that. Let me demonstrate.

Flip through this book and you'll see the explanations to 34 different tricks. Or, I should say, that's the illusion. What you're really seeing are the plots to 34 different one-act plays. They should all, even the simplest of them, be performed with as much pizzazz as you can squeeze in.

If you just do these tricks, you'll miss the whole point. It would be like telling a joke from the punch line up. The importance of The Show is the key point to keep in mind as you read the rest of this book, because there's a natural tendency to look at each trick for nothing but the secret that makes it work. Actually, the "secret" is the easiest part to the trick.

You can generally learn that in an instant. Then you have to learn the technique, and that often takes a little longer.

But finally, you have to learn a presentation. And that's the heart and soul.

And how does one learn how to "present" a trick? What's the secret to The Show?

The secret is simple. High quality, believable lying. It's the key skill to razzmatazz presentation. And I'm not talking about wimpy little fibs. I'm talking about WHOPPERS! Horrendous lies! Lies told with enormous enthusiasm, big gestures and a clear, steady gaze.

I know what you're saying at this point, because I said the same thing: "How can a rare person like myself — lacking a dishonest cell in my body — how can I possibly even get my tongue to say these awful things?" All I can say is

⭐ Try it. You'd be amazed.

The Magician's
BLOOD OATH

I once attended a college party where I had a chance to watch a Small Human Drama enacted. A freshman at the party, obviously not a member of the fraternity, was standing on the sidelines forlornly waiting for a break in the social weather. He had come by himself and it looked very much as if he was going to stay that way. His situation was clearly desperate when he suddenly buttonholed one of the caterers and began performing a magic trick.

Fortunately, it was not a bad one and he clearly had practiced it. As it went on, a little crowd began to gather around him, hoping to figure it out when the grand finale came.

Fortunately, he managed to pull it off and fooled them, one and all. For a moment, it looked as if he might have saved his social day. And then he blew it. He had nothing to follow it with and when the crowd bore in on him for the secret, he gave it away. There were groans all around when he revealed that there were actually two bracelets, not just one. Suddenly, it wasn't magic anymore, it was nothing but a cheap trick, and like millions of amateur magicians before him, the freshman discovered:

THE BIGGEST LAW IN MAGIC:
Everybody loves a good piece of magic, but nobody likes a cheap trick.

**IN ORDER TO READ
THE REST OF THIS BOOK
YOU MUST TAKE THE**

MAGICIAN'S BLOOD OATH

I hereby promise to:

Never ever repeat a trick

and

Never give it away.

PS: If they really, really, really want to know how you did it… just use the magic words, "Let me show you something a little different."

May I cut off your
PINKY?

Your volunteer extends a pinky. You wrap a cord around it and jerk tight, threatening to cut off the finger. Instead — instantly, invisibly — the string is off the finger, which remains attached to the hand.

1

Just drape the string over the right-hand pinky like so...

Right hand

Grab a volunteer. Explain how this is probably going to hurt like crazy, but hey, that's show biz. Ask him to point his **right-hand** pinky at you. Then wrap your cord around it as indicated. Look carefully at the illustration and wrap exactly right. Any mistakes at this point could be painful.

...then take one turn around the finger. KEY POINT! Use your victim's right hand and wrap exactly as per the illustration! Don't mess this part up!

Right hand

2

Once the cord is properly in place explain to your volunteer that he should stare at his finger for the last time. **"Relax. Let your pinky go absolutely limp. Otherwise** (lower your voice) **there could be problems."**

3 Grab both ends, close your eyes, and pull the string tight. Gasp if you like. If you wrapped right, the string will bend the finger, allowing the loops to slip off. It happens in the blink of an eye. If you don't wrap right, you'll pull in the direction that the finger doesn't bend. Then the loops won't slip off, the volunteer will grab his finger and holler and — worst of all — the trick won't work.

Get ready to pull in these directions.

Hold the string out like so, remind your victim to keep his pinky limp...

End up like this.

...then pull tight with a single, quick motion.

4 Hopefully though, you got it right. The finger will bend (as it's designed to), the loops will slip off, and the finger will snap back straight, all before anyone can see what happened.

P.S. One refinement: As you pull the string tight, simultaneously push it in a little bit toward your victim. If you do that, after the snap, you'll end up with the string pressed into the webbing between pinky and ring finger. That's a strong finishing visual image that strengthens the "penetration" effect.

P.P.S. Practice this one with someone who trusts you before you take it public. And pull the string gently.

Young Clips

In Love

This is one of those rare tricks that is
a lot more fun to do than watch. As a result,
the best way to "perform" it is to simply
demonstrate the moves to someone else once or
twice, and then let her try it. You'll need a dollar bill
and some paper clips. Try as they might,
I don't think anyone can muff this trick.

Clip your dollar bill back on itself
in a Z-shape with the paper clips.

Second clip

First clip

Hold your folded bill up and
announce that these paper clips are
young and in love and are looking
for a way to make a meaningful
commitment to one another.

Bird's Eye View

Second clip

First clip

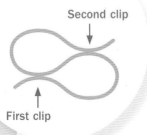

Grab
here.

Grab
here.

Then snap the dollar bill straight out. The clips will link together and fly straight up (front-row spectators beware!). If you're smooth, you'll catch the clips on their way down and reveal the fact that they are now married together.

Happy ending.

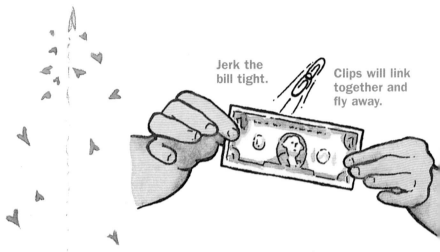

Jerk the bill tight.

Clips will link together and fly away.

"Look, Ma!
I'm a magician!"

Separate the clips, hand them and the dollar over to your nearest spectator and walk her through it. She should be happily linking clips in no time.

THE BROOM AND EGG

Probably the best no-skill big trick in the known world.
You'll need a broom, three eggs and a few other common things.
Go find them. This is worth it.

- One broom
- One pie tin
- Three raw eggs

- Three half-full plastic drinking glasses

- Three cardboard tubes (the kind you find inside toilet paper rolls)

1 Set up on the edge of a table, as in the illustration. Clear out the area behind all this apparatus, because in a minute the pie tin is going to be flying. Make sure the eggs are big enough so that they "perch" on top of the tubes rather than wedge into them.

Line up each egg directly over the middle of each water glass. This is key.

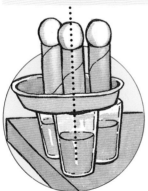

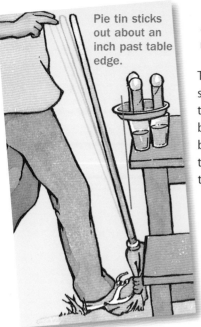

Pie tin sticks out about an inch past table edge.

2 If you've set up right, the pie tin overhangs the table by an inch.

That overhanging edge is your target. Try to hit it square on. Put the business end of the broom on the floor directly below the tin and tromp on the bristles. Now you should have a "spring-loaded" broom — ready to whap. When you haul it back toward you, your trick is cocked. If you let go of the broom, it'll whap the pie tin.

3 Close your eyes, count to three, and let go.

When the dust settles, the pie tin and cardboard tubes should be everywhere, but the three eggs should be resting comfortably inside the half-filled glasses.

If you do everything wrong, pie tin, glasses, eggs, etc. will go flying, as pictured below. But even that's pretty funny.

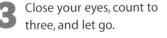

Another high-speed trick for the magician on the go.
It has a great eye-rubbing effect, but it's very fast and
very easy. You can do it with your string, but it looks
a little better with bigger rope, like clothesline.

The THREAD *and the* NEEDLE

Using about two or three feet of rope or string, wrap it around your thumb EXACTLY as illustrated. Take this part slow.

The loop

Tell the audience you want to thread this "needle" (the loop). But you're lying. What you're really going to do is miss to the outside.

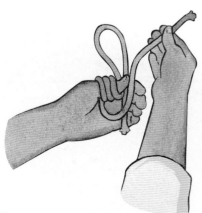

◀ Grab the dangling end and take aim at the loop. With a quick stabbing motion, fake as if you put the end of the rope through the loop. In reality, miss to the outside.

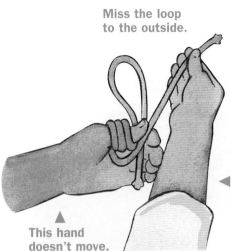

Miss the loop to the outside.

This is a hard move to illustrate, but an easy move to do. If the illustrations are confusing, try this. Pretend you are horribly nearsighted but are going to try to thread both your hand and your end of the rope through the small loop. This is clearly impossible, but you're nearsighted. You can't tell.

◀ **This hand moves quickly in a stabbing motion.**

▲ **This hand doesn't move.**

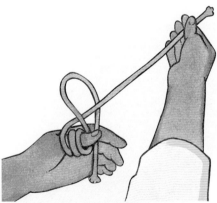

You take a deep breath and go for it. Unfortunately, you're off to the outside of the loop by an inch or so, but you don't even realize it. You keep on going until you get to the end of the rope. Then, lo and behold, you put on your glasses and you've done it, the rope is through the loop. Amazing.

And you're done!

PS: The key to the trick is in the threading motion. Try it slowly at first. Aim for the loop, go for it, miss by an inch to the outside but keep going. As you come to the end of your rope, it will slide along the bottom of the wraps on your thumb and then slip into the loop through its bottom. Do it fast and it's a visual impossibility.

A POCKETFUL OF Fraud

Here's the effect: The magician pulls out a handful of change, takes a coin from it, returns the rest of the change to his pocket and then tosses the single coin from one hand to the other. Holding the coin inside his extended fist, he asks the audience "Heads or Tails?" Then, he opens his hand to reveal... no coin. Naturally everyone suspects the other hand, but when he opens that one... no coin there either.

This is just practice. Do it by yourself.

1 Reach into your pocket, pull out a handful of change, and display it to your imaginary audience.

2 With your other hand, select a single coin and put the rest back in your pocket. Don't make a big production out of this. Just do it very naturally.

Hold the coin in such a way that your fingers conceal it from your audience.

3 Now throw the coin hard from one hand to the other. Really zing it — a straight line bullet that hits your other hand hard enough to make a small slapping sound.

4 Then repeat the whole process from step one. Do this practice run until you're bored. It usually doesn't take long.

A little more practice
(but this time, fake the whole thing)

1 Start exactly as before. Reach into your pocket and pull out some change.

But this time FAKE IT. Don't take a thing. Just make sure your movements look exactly as they did before.

Hold the coin up just like before. Only this time there's no coin.

2 Then keep right on going. Fake the zingy little throw. And here's the most important part, and the one that'll take a little practice. You've got to fake that little slapping sound. In order to do that, loosen your fingers up and slap them onto the heel of your palm as you "catch" the coin. If you can get that sound right, you're home free.

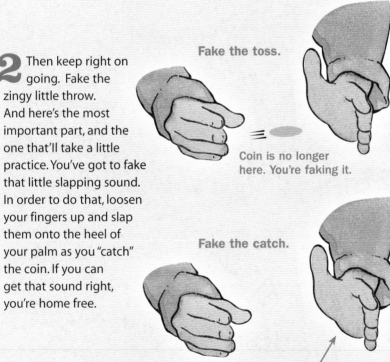

Fake the toss.

Coin is no longer here. You're faking it.

Fake the catch.

Close this hand with a clapping noise.

P.S. **Practice both ways. Do it with a real coin, then fake it — no coin. When the two look and sound identical, you're ready for your audience.**

Pick up a coin. Show it off.
Take it in your other hand... and it's gone.
Vanished. This is the foundation move to magic.
Non-optional.

THEFRENCHDROP

Half-dollars are best so you should snag the next one that goes by, but in the meantime, use a quarter. Hold it as shown on the facing page.

Look at the illustrations and practice *actually* passing the coin from one hand to the next. Don't do anything funny. Just act naturally and watch your hands carefully. What you are looking at is a perfect French Drop. Memorize reality and then keep it in mind as you begin to fake it. Magic nirvana is when reality and the fake are absolutely identical. At that point, not even the magician knows if he has actually passed the coin or not.

Do the real thing for practice.

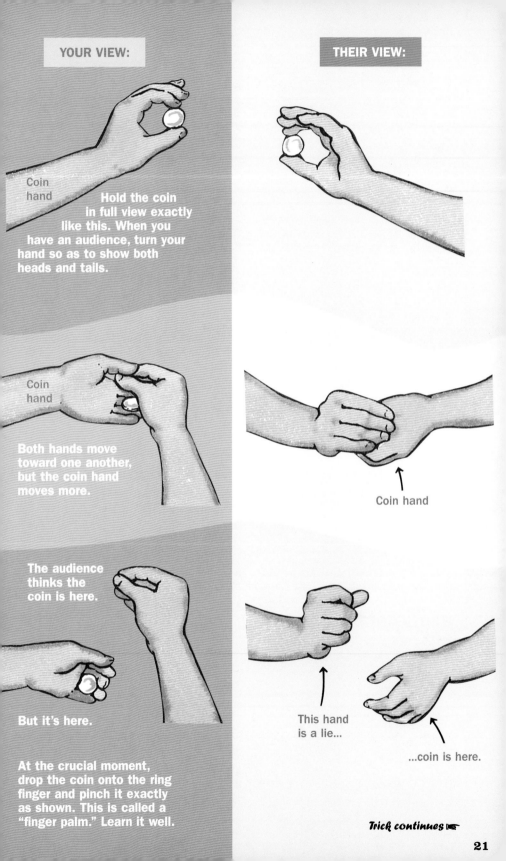

Coin hand

Hold the coin in full view exactly like this. When you have an audience, turn your hand so as to show both heads and tails.

Coin hand

Both hands move toward one another, but the coin hand moves more.

Coin hand

The audience thinks the coin is here.

But it's here.

At the crucial moment, drop the coin onto the ring finger and pinch it exactly as shown. This is called a "finger palm." Learn it well.

This hand is a lie...

...coin is here.

Trick continues ☞

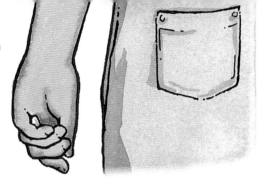

After the drop, let your coin hand fall to your side. Keep that hand as boring as possible. Don't clench it. Don't pay any attention to it. A good finger palm will enable you to keep your fingers loose and natural.

Bring your clenched empty hand up into full view. This is the hand that "contains" the coin. You must believe that very deeply. If you do, so will your audience. Stare at it. Move it around. You are now acting.

How to Make Your French Drop Look Perfect

Learning the French Drop is like learning to whistle.
It's easy to get the basics, just a minute or two. But perfection... that's a bit different. The reality is it takes practice. Make it a rule never to stand in line again without practicing your French Drop. Here are some points to keep in mind.

- The hand that holds the coin should move much more than the hand that receives it.
- You should be putting the coin into place, not reaching out to take it.
- As you practice, keep going back and forth between "reality" and the fake.
- Drop the coin at the exact instant you appear to be grabbing it.
- Remember, in this trick, half-seconds count. Practice until you feel confident and slick. That's the point at which you can start to fool people.

How to Make Your French Drop Into a Tasteless Trick

By itself, the French Drop is just a small gotcha.
But you can enlarge it very simply to make a little trick.

Let's say you've just finished a French Drop. Your audience thinks the coin is in your clenched hand. But don't open it to reveal their mistake. Instead, put your empty hand to your mouth and noisily suck the "coin" out of it. Bug out your eyes and fake a big swallow, Glunk. Next, pass the coin through your digestive tract. You will need to make weird facial expressions while this happens.

Finally, reach around behind yourself (with the hand that does have the coin in it) and make a squawking noise, like a chicken laying an egg.

Finally, bring the coin around. Show it off. Ask if anyone would like to inspect it. And burp.

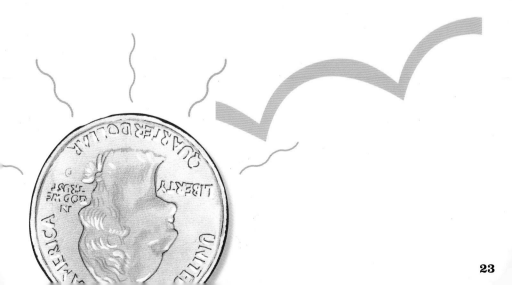

Where's the Rub?

A quarter is lying on the table. You pick it up, rub it on your arm and it's gone. Vanished.

1 You'll need a quarter, a table to sit at, and a good story.

2 Roll up your sleeves, and pick up the quarter (with your right hand). Show it to the audience and announce, briefly: **"Quarter."** *Hand the quarter over to your left hand,* put your chin on your right hand and begin rubbing the quarter into your exposed arm. Hold the quarter in such a way that it is not visible, then, in your most convincing voice, start talking…

Coin is here.

"About fifteen or twenty years ago, they began making quarters out of melted-down pennies… just using a copper core and coating it… if you rub hard enough, the salt in your perspiration can start a reaction that rubs off the thin silvering… and you'll get a copper quarter!… shows you how low things have gotten these days… sandwich quarters… used to make them solid silver, back when men were men… blah blah blah…"

This goes on for the whole trick. That's what your mouth is doing. Meanwhile, here's what your hands should be up to.

Quarter has "slipped."

3 Almost immediately, after one or two rubs, the quarter should "slip" out of your fingers and drop onto the table. *Don't stop talking!*

Take your chin off your hand, pick up the quarter with your "chin hand," and fake the pass back to your "rubbing hand" — and go right back to rubbing. This incredibly brazen move has got to be smooth, smooth, smooth. If you feel guilty about this fake, you'll never get away with it.

Pick it up...

...fake the handoff...

The pass should be an identical fake of the pass you opened the trick with. **Key Point:** Keep eye contact with your audience and don't let your story skip a beat. You want them looking in your deep blue eyes, not staring at your shifty hands.

Coin stays in this hand.

4 Now for the fun part. Rub for a while longer, stop once to bring your hand up to "look" at your coin, and keep the story rolling. After a while, start frowning. (**"Something's gone wrong..."**) Drop the audience eye contact and look at your rubbing hand. Rub a little harder.

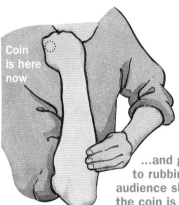

Coin is here now

...and go back to rubbing. The audience should think the coin is in here.

Then suddenly brighten up. Slow down the rubbing and begin lifting your fingers one by one very slowly. No quarter! Where'd it go? That's easy. You dropped it down your shirt collar when everyone was looking at your empty rubbing hand. Hold both hands out empty and smile.

"That's funny. I guess the whole thing rubbed away."

Lindbergh's
HANKIE

You put a quarter into the middle of a white hankie.
A volunteer presses on it. You pick up
the hankie and the coin is gone.
Impossible? Actually, it's
pretty easy.

1 You'll need a white handkerchief, a dime and a bar of white soap, or you can buy a pack of stickum at the hardware store.

2 Before you call in your audience, cut a little sliver of soap and mash it onto one corner of the hankie. Call in your audience (keep them in front of you) and spread out the hankie on a table in front of you. The soap should be invisible.

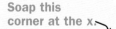
Soap this corner at the x

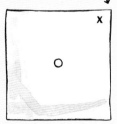

3 Lay the dime in the center of the hankie. Explain that you have never done this trick before. You're not sure what is supposed to happen.

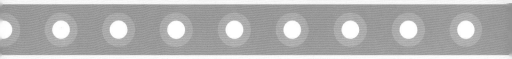

4 Lay the four corners of the hankie down onto the dime, one at a time. Key Point: Start with the soaped corner.

Get volunteer
to press here.

x   x   x

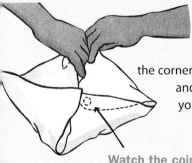

5 Ask a volunteer to confirm that the dime is still there by pressing on it. Make sure he or she presses hard enough to stick the dime to the soap.

6 Look at the illustrations carefully for this part. Put your hands back to back, insert your fingers into the crease nearest you and simultaneously spread the hankie as you lift it into a vertically displayed position. Do this move snappily. As you do it, the coin should stick to the corner of the hankie and slide right into your hand.

Watch the coin.

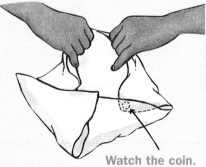

Watch the coin.

Coin hides here.

7 Display your hankie at the edge of the table so you can drop the coin behind it onto your lap. Show both sides of the hankie and show both hands empty.

27

the
BEST TRICK
in this
book

Here's the effect:
It's very simple.
It's very impossible.
A volunteer touches
a coin. As they do,
while their finger *is
actually on the coin*,
it disappears.

Mind-altering.

You'll need the small square of latex that is stuck on the back of the book. Because the latex is so thin, you'll only get eight or nine usages out of it before it tears, so be very careful with it.

The execution of the trick is so simple, you only need to practice it once. After that you've got six or seven performances left so choose your audiences carefully. Don't waste this trick on ingrates. (P.S. You can order more squares from www.klutz.com.)

Do this set-up phase out of sight of your audience.

Place a quarter on the end of a small cylinder, like a lipstick container. Stretch the latex in all four directions (north/south/east/ west) until it's see-through thin and press it over the quarter. Then bring your hands together under the quarter and gently release.

Stretch the latex over the quarter...

If you've done it right, an amazing thing will happen. The quarter will "seal" into the center of the square. It will look as if it's on the top side (the latex is so thin as to be invisible), but in truth it will be on the bottom side.

...bring in thumbs and release.

Then place the latex (with quarter embedded) over the top of a clear glass. Quarter on the underside (looks like it's on the top side, right?). Use a rubber band to keep the latex stretched in place. Set the glass down and don't allow it to be moved. Now you're all set.

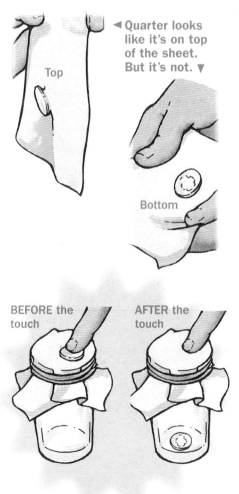

◄ Quarter looks like it's on top of the sheet. But it's not. ▼

Top

Bottom

BEFORE the touch

AFTER the touch

Bring in the audience and do the show.

Have them look the situation over, but no touching please. Ask a volunteer to step forward and give them the following instructions: "You are about to witness one of the few miracles left on this planet. On the count of three, please press quickly on this quarter. And watch carefully, this only happens once a lifetime."

Bingo! The quarter pops into the glass and you never even touched it. Now for the tough part. **DON'T DO IT AGAIN!** No matter what they say. Do your next trick and don't look back.

VANISHING SALT SHAKER

A quarter sits on the table in front of you. You put a salt shaker over it. Pull the shaker away... to reveal the coin's still there, it's the shaker that's disappeared.

You and your audience will need to be sitting at a table. (A restaurant booth is ideal.) Before you announce this trick, shuffle around so that no one has a clear view of your lap. You'll need a fresh napkin, coin and salt shaker.

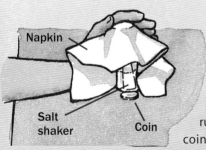

Napkin

Salt shaker

Coin

Announce that you are going to try a little coin magic. By rubbing the coin with the bottom of a salt shaker, you think you can make the coin disappear. You saw this once on TV. Place a coin in front of you on the table. Cover the shaker with a napkin.

IMPORTANT: Cover the shaker tightly, so that the napkin clings to the shaker and takes on the shape of it, like a napkin "shell."

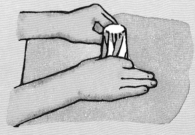

This hand needs to be ready to move.

Rub shaker over coin... and as you pull shaker away...

Hold the covered shaker at its base and begin slowly rubbing it over the coin. Say the magic words... **"Please please please please disappear."**

...quickly cover coin with hand

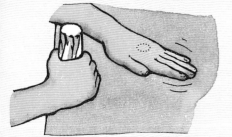

After four or five rubs, get ready to do two things quickly: One, move the covered shaker toward you, and two, slap your other hand down onto the coin *before anyone can see if it's there or not.* Then slowly lift your hand. Disappointingly, the coin is still there. Look pained.

and move shaker to edge.

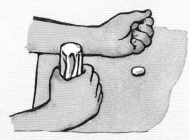

Put back the covered shaker and rub some more. Say the magic words even harder. Move the shaker toward you again, and once again slap down your other hand over the coin before anyone can see if it's there. Set the shaker down away from the coin.

Reveal coin.

Rub shaker over coin.

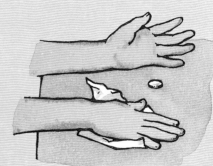

Cover coin with hand.

Drop shaker into lap.

Then slowly (very slowly) lift your hand to reveal… that the coin is still there. Hang your head in shame. Curse the forces of evil while slamming your fist onto the covered salt shaker — which, incidentally, has disappeared, leaving only a squashed napkin "shell."

Reveal coin.

There's no shaker here. Only a napkin shell. The shaker is on your lap.

Squash the "shaker" flat.

Trick continues ☞

How did you do that?

Easy. The second time you removed the salt shaker, when you slapped your hand over the coin, your other hand was dropping the shaker onto your lap. When you put the "shaker" back on the table, you did it very carefully so that no one could tell the napkin shell was all that was left.

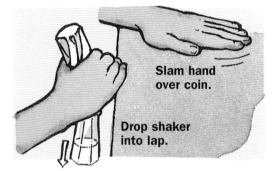

Slam hand over coin.

Drop shaker into lap.

P.S. Note one important point. The first time you remove the shaker, move it toward you, almost to the edge of the table. That way, the second time, when you do take it all the way off the edge, nothing will seem out of the ordinary.

WEIRD GRAVITY COINS

A coin vanishes from one hand
and reappears in the other.
Then, as your audience is
trying to figure <u>that</u> out,
it happens <u>again</u>!

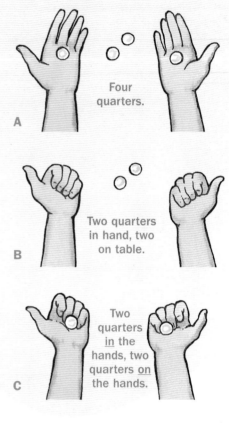

Four quarters.

A

1 Sit down at a table and lay four
quarters in front of you. Put your hands on
the table beside them. Open, palm up. Take
a deep breath, you are about to begin lying.

"Here are four quarters and two empty
hands. Please count them carefully. Please
put one quarter in each of my hands. Thank
you. Good volunteers are hard to find these
days. Observe as I close my hands very
carefully, very lovingly, around the quarters."

Two quarters
in hand, two
on table.

B

"Now. Carefully. Slowly. Place the other
two quarters ON TOP of my hands. This
is a critical step. Please do it carefully."
(Whisper this part.)

Two
quarters
<u>in</u> the
hands, two
quarters <u>on</u>
the hands.

C

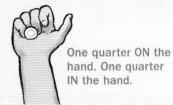

One quarter ON the hand. One quarter IN the hand.

One quarter ON the hand. One quarter IN the hand.

2 Stare at the two showing coins for a second and then say: **"No. Actually, I'd like you to do it the other way. Can you just swap the top quarters?"** Turn your hands over, and the two quarters on top of your hands fall to the table. Your volunteer picks them up again and replaces them as they were, except swapping them left for right, as you requested.

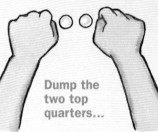

Dump the two top quarters...

...let your volunteer put them back.

3 This step is easy. Open your fingers just a tad and "swallow" the two top quarters into your hands.

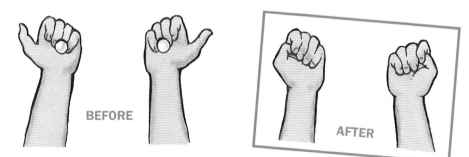

BEFORE

AFTER

The Payoff

Your audience — assuming they've been watching — thinks that each of your hands contains two quarters. You should ask them: "How many quarters are in my hands?"

When they say ...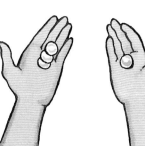
open both hands.
One hand contains
three; the other
hand, one.

How You Pulled the Fast One

Go back to Step 2. When you dumped the top coins, you cheated.
One hand "swallowed" its top coin; the other hand dumped
BOTH its coins.

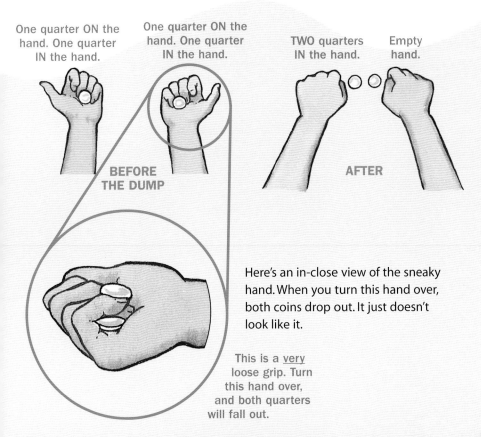

One quarter ON the hand. One quarter IN the hand.

One quarter ON the hand. One quarter IN the hand.

TWO quarters IN the hand.

Empty hand.

BEFORE THE DUMP

AFTER

Here's an in-close view of the sneaky hand. When you turn this hand over, both coins drop out. It just doesn't look like it.

This is a very loose grip. Turn this hand over, and both quarters will fall out.

This is nice and showy. It's a large trick that needs volunteers, and works well for a crowd. Pull it out the next time you're put in front of an angry mob of five-year-old birthday party animals.

SIAMESE TWIN ROPES

1 You'll need three volunteers, two pieces of rope, a bandana or hankie and a short length of secret thread. Cotton clothesline works well for the rope, and for the secret thread, something that matches the color of the rope.

2 Do this part away from prying eyes: Grab both pieces of rope (they should be about five feet long) right at their midpoints. Then, using your secret thread, tie them together with a little loop right at that point.

The ropes are now linked at their centers. ("Siamese Ropes"... get it?) Hold both ropes so that your hand covers the secret loop and bring on the audience.

3 Explain that you are going to expose the old "saw-the-poor-lady-in-half" trick by doing it with rope and ("So that you can see what actually happens!") you're going to do it in full view. You don't care what other magicians think, you're going to expose this shabby trick once and for all.

4 Collar three volunteers from the audience and march them up front. Display the ropes freely. If your magic thread is anywhere near the right color, it will be invisible and you don't have to worry too much about concealing the loop. Just handle the two in such a way that the fact of their "Siamese Twinness" is not obvious.

5 As you're maneuvering the ropes, you'll have to pull off the only real "move" of the trick, but it's quite easy. As you're holding the ropes at their mid-point, choose a good moment to drop your hand to your side as you do the following: Insert your forefinger between the two ropes and rotate them so that you end up holding two "U's" tied together at their midpoints. (Look at the illustrations!)

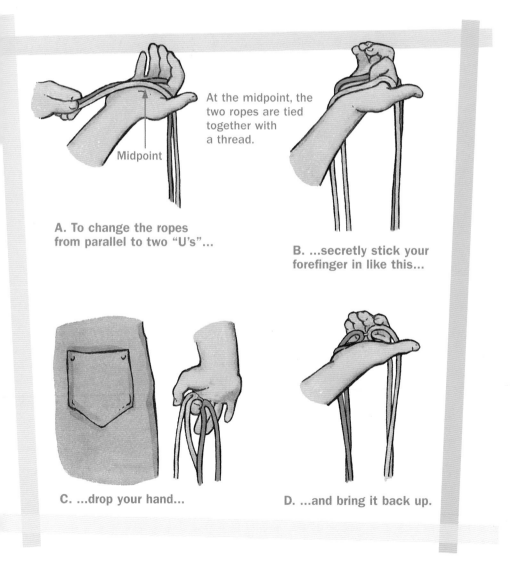

At the midpoint, the two ropes are tied together with a thread.

Midpoint

A. To change the ropes from parallel to two "U's"...

B. ...secretly stick your forefinger in like this...

C. ...drop your hand...

D. ...and bring it back up.

Trick continues ☞

6 What you've accomplished, very simply, is this: The two ropes which had been running parallel to one another, are now in the shape of two "U's" and the only thing holding them together is a little piece of thread. Now, clearly, you'll have to keep that thread covered, so keep your hand over it. From the audience's point of view, nothing has changed (little do they know...).

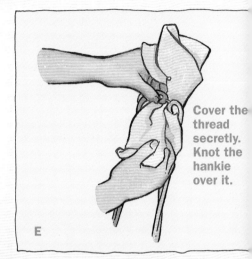

Cover the thread secretly. Knot the hankie over it.

E

7 Explain to your audience that you want to keep these two ropes from falling apart so you're going to tie them together. Then pull out your hankie and knot it over the telltale thread. Practice a bit so that you can do this without looking as if you're doing what you're actually doing.

8 Now ask your volunteers who among them would like to be the "sawers" and who would like to be the "sawee." Once they've settled that, position the "sawers" to either side of the "sawee." Place the two ropes as illustrated across the "sawee's" tummy, with the hankie over the belly button region.

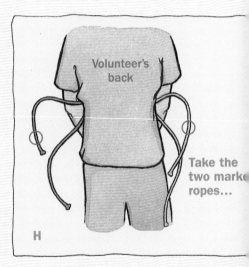

Volunteer's back

Take the two marke ropes...

H

9 You're going to tie these ropes behind your volunteer, so turn him around so everyone can see what you're doing at his back. Take only the top two ropes and cross them in a simple overhand knot, then hand each of the "sawers" two ends of the rope as illustrated. (Make sure you get this part right. If you don't, big problems.)

10 Now rotate your little threesome back again so they're facing the audience. If you haven't muffed anything, the audience thinks one rope passes in front of your "sawee" and one behind him. He's stuck in the middle.

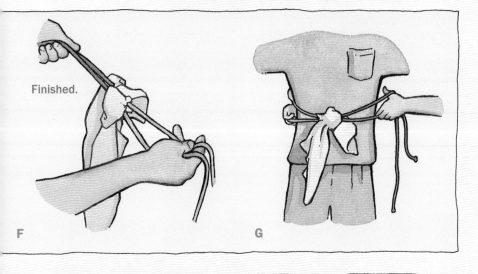

Finished.

F

G

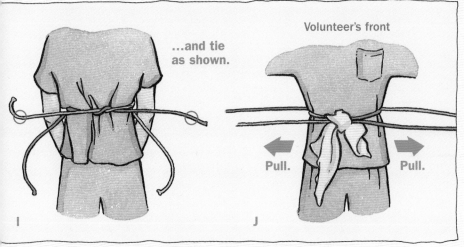

...and tie
as shown.

Volunteer's front

Pull.   Pull.

I

J

11 Explain that this part takes a little effort (*"It depends on the exact location of certain internal organs. It's a little different for everybody."* Rummage around in your volunteer's ribs a little at this point). You are going to pass these ropes through the center part of this poor person's "corpus medici." If it's done quickly enough…*"it is often pain-free."*

12 On the count of three, both outside volunteers pull hard, the thread breaks, the two ropes appear suddenly intact behind the "sawee" and both volunteers still have their ends. Not bad.

I once broke the cardinal rule of magic and did this trick more than once. It was on a beach, in the evening, for an audience of 14 Boy Scouts. By the third go-round, they all had their noses and flashlights six inches from my hands when I had to pull off the single move that the trick requires. And they still didn't catch it. That moment could have been the highlight of my magic career.

Rope
Handcuffs

1 Probably the best way to start this trick is with two hapless volunteers. Tie their wrists together as illustrated and then give them two minutes to extricate themselves. The rules say you can't untie the ropes, but all sorts of embarrassing contortions are perfectly fine. Ideally, they will tie themselves into hopeless knots.

2 Two minutes later. They've given up. You and your assistant agree to switch places with them. You may allow anyone to tie your wrists together, but make sure that one of your assistant's wrists has just a little bit of breathing room. It doesn't take much, but don't let them cut off the circulation. The knots can be as elaborate and bullet-proof as humanly possible.

To get out, follow these steps.

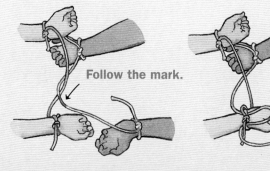

Follow the mark.

3 Proceed to tie your bodies into a hopeless knot. Roll on the ground if necessary. When your hands are buried in the middle of all this, out of sight, push the middle of your rope through your assistant's wrist loop and then over his hand. Look at the illustration below carefully for this bit. Do it wrong and you'll come out double-tied, not untied. All your assistant has to do is go limp and be cooperative.

4 That's it. The two of you are now unconnected, although nobody knows it yet. At this point, it's all show, so take your time. Grunt and groan, twist and shout, roll around… finally, untangle yourselves and… step free! (**"Anybody else want to try?"**)

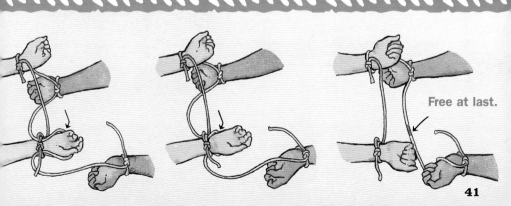

Free at last.

41

Gypsy Switch

Like the French Drop, the Gypsy Switch can be done either as a small piece of magic by itself, or it can be incorporated into larger tricks. It is very old, very easy, and very, very good. You'll need a bandana or hankie, a couple of paper clips, and a volunteer who can come up with a dollar bill.

1 First off, a bit of preparation. Write the words "Five Dollars" on a 3"x5" index card. Fold it two or three times and use a paper clip to keep it from unfolding, then put it in your right pocket. Drop a second paper clip into your left pocket and bring in an audience.

Five Dollars

2 Produce your bandana from a pocket with a flourish and pass it around for inspection. Then reach into your pocket looking for a dollar bill. Unfortunately, you're all out. Ask someone else for a little assistance. (**"More of an investment than a loan."**) When someone finally comes up with a bill, reach both hands into your pockets for a paper clip. With your right hand, palm the folded 3x5 card, with your left hand come up with the clip.

3 Give your rich volunteer the clip and ask him to fold his bill two or three times and clip it shut. Meanwhile, the bandana has come back to you. Spread it over your open right hand, the one containing the palmed 3x5 card. The act of spreading the hankie conceals the card.

4 Place the bill into the center of the bandana, on your palm. Finally, explain what you are going to do. Incredibly enough, you are going to turn this single into a five. Look at the illustrations for this part. If you've set up right, the bill has been placed into the center of the hankie which is spread over your right hand. Directly underneath the bill — and underneath the bandana — is the folded card. **Key Point:** The bill and card have to be lined up exactly on top of one another.

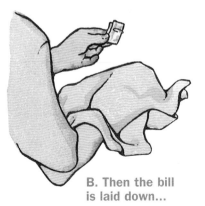

Dollar

Card

YOUR PROPS

A. Lay the bandana over the concealed card.

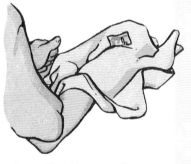

C. ...directly over the concealed card.

B. Then the bill is laid down...

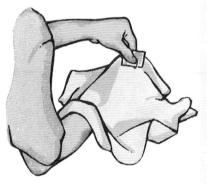

D. Key Move: Pick up the bill, the bandana, and the card, all in one smooth move.

5 This is the crucial step. Look at the illustrations and practice carefully. Pick up the bill, the 3x5, and the hankie all in one smooth move. Twist the hankie once or twice around the 3x5 card, palm the bill in your right hand and return the hankie with your left to the former owner of the bill. Drop your guilty hand to your side and explain that this is where it gets tricky.

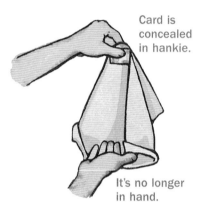

Card is concealed in hankie.

It's no longer in hand.

E. Replace the bandana, bill and card...

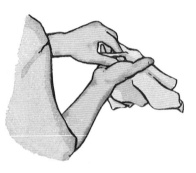

G. ...back onto your palm and...

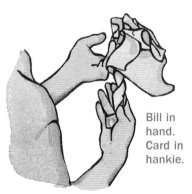

Bill in hand. Card in hankie.

F. ...begin twisting the card into the bandana...

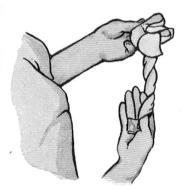

H. ...as you palm the bill. Hand the hankie over as you secretly pocket the bill.

Five Dollars

6 Your volunteer is clutching the
twisted hankie with their "bill" inside it. Now,
very earnestly, give them the following instructions:
**"Stare at your bill inside that hankie. Warm it by rubbing
it on your cheek. Inhale its aroma deeply. Dream about it.
Wish with all your might that it could grow and grow and
grow into a great big FIVE dollar bill."**

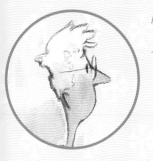

7 During this little performance, you should pocket the
bill. Your excuse for going to your pocket can be to find
a penny to drop into the hankie so as to "fertilize" the
bill. Whether you come up with one or not doesn't really
matter. The spectator is still holding their "bill" so their
suspicions aren't up yet.

8 Now you're ready. Tell the spectator to
slowly remove his "bill" from the hankie. **("If
you've been good, your wish has been granted.")**
When they come up with their "five," get all excited
("You got your wish! Isn't that special!").

the
MAGIC EGG

Some of the tricks in this book are 60% show and 40% trick. Some are 80% show and 20% trick. But there's only one that's 99% show and 1% trick...

1 Equipment required? One paper lunchbag. Practice required? Hold it as shown. Snap your fingers and the bag should jerk (without falling out of your hand). Try it once or twice to get the feel. You are now done with all the necessary practice.

2 Reach into your pocket and find an invisible egg. Toss it high into the air and then run around and try to catch it in the bag. If you succeed, the bag will jerk and you'll hear the egg as it hits the bottom of the bag. If it doesn't jerk, and you hear no sound, it's because you didn't read the paragraph before this one and you didn't snap your fingers. Try again. Now you are ready for your audience and ready to tell your story.

3 Reach into your pocket and rummage around. Pull an invisible egg out and hold it up for inspection. Get a volunteer to stand next to you.

"I have in my hands here an invisible egg. Would you like to see it? Yes? Well, you can't. It's invisible. You're not listening."

Toss it up and "catch" it in the bag. Toss it up a little higher and repeat. Finally zing it hard to the bag, two or three times. After every catch, discreetly snap your fingers for convincing visual and sound effects.

"It's easy. Try it. Just don't drop."

Hand it to your volunteer and let them try. A couple of quick tosses that you "catch" every time.

4 "You're pretty good… but can you do it from 3-point land?" Back off and when they throw it, DON'T snap your fingers as you "watch" it sail over the bag and splat on the ground. Pause. Look at the volunteer. Sigh. Reach into your pocket for another one and rummage around unsuccessfully.

"Do you have one?" ask the volunteer. They'll either try to hand you a new invisible egg (in which case, go over, look at it, try to touch it and then say disgustedly, "There's nothing here! Who you trying to fool!").

More likely though, your volunteer will just look blankly at you. Then you should have an idea. Do this:

Tell them to put their hands into their underarms, extend their neck and flap their "wings" while saying "bukk bukk BAAAAAH!" As they do that, run around behind them and look at their… egg producing area. Make them cluck a little louder then suddenly grab an invisible egg as it falls toward the ground. "Got it!"

Give it to them again and this time, when they throw it at the bag from far away "catch" it with a finger snap. Run up, stand beside your volunteer and the two of you should take a deep bow, clucking all the while.

P.S. And when you've read this whole book and can start doing birthday parties, now would be the time to reach into the bag and pull out the baby chick which you slipped in during all the previous shenanigans.

THE GREAT
AMERICAN
Nasal Band

Have you ever wanted to inhale a whole rubber band? Through your nose?

Like most kids, your answer to that question was probably "Of course! Who wouldn't?"

Who wouldn't indeed? With that in mind, here's our very special rubber band inhalation system.

Stretch the band and hold it like so. A regular tan rubberband is best.

1 Equipment needed: one rubber band of the regular size. Look at the pictures and practice. Hook it on your pinky, stretch it as shown, close your hand around it, and by letting go it snaps back into your hand and, from the audience's point of view, vanishes.

Now bring in the audience. Show that you have nothing in your hands and start a drum roll, **"Check this out!"** Reach into your pocket and produce your rubber band with a big TA-DA! **"Hey! Come on! It's not every magician who travels with his own band!"**

Close your fingers.

Let go of the band. It snaps back into your hand.

Do a few finger exercises with your rubber band while you talk about how special it is. Show how you can leap short buildings **"with a single band!"** (Demonstrate this by shooting it straight up and catching.)

"But its most amazing power… it can even block your nasal passages!"

2 Demonstrate by holding the band just like you practiced, stretched in your hand. The audience doesn't see that it's stretched, only that an inch or two extends from the top of your hand.

Hold it near your nose and give a huge snort while throwing your head back. Vanish the band by letting it snap back into your hand. Do it right, and it will appear as if you've snorted the band right up your nose. Smile and sniffle a little bit.

"I hab this strange tickling beeling…"

3 Then comes a big sneeze. Cover your face politely and suddenly out of your hand and into view drops the rubber band, although still hooked to your pinky so it just dangles down from your hand.

"What? You don't believe? Want to take a closer look?" Push your nose up so you look like a pig and ask if anyone would like to look inside.

"Or maybe you'd like to inspect the rubber band…" and try to hand it around.

Right about now would probably be a good time for the next trick.

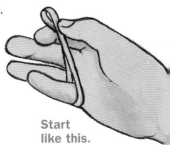

Start like this.

PSYCHIC
Silverware

This is one of the most universally popular pranks with moms everywhere. Just imagine your own mother's delight as she watches you bend her favorite silverware on the edge of the dining room table.

With nothing but the power of your astonishing psycho-kinetic mental powers — and your lying tongue — you will be able to bend a straight fork in front of your audience's disbelieving eyes. You're sitting at the table with your family and friends. Grab a fork and (secretly) hold it and a dime in both hands as shown in The Set Up. Place the tines against the edge of the table and bring everyone's attention to it. Grunt and groan while you fake-bend it. Show a sliver of dime at the top (looks like the top of the fork) and this fake-bend looks terrific. Before mom can even holler at you, tell everyone to be totally silent.

Close your eyes, hold your breath, and concentrate on the fork (still concealed in your hand). Then, with a flourish, open your hands.

Normal fork! No bend!

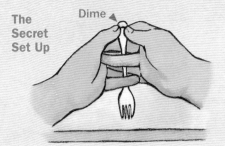

The
Secret
Set Up

Dime

This is What It Looks Like You're Doing

This is What You're Really Doing

Dime

Hold...

Dime

...and (fake) bend.

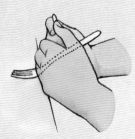

Note: Trick only works for people sitting opposite you at the table. Those to your side can see too much.

Hold the dime firmly and let the fork slide.

THUMBS UP
RING RELEASE

Another member of the Magic Hall of Fame, Oldtimers Division. It's a magic quickie that works best if done in combination with one or two of the other string and ring tricks.

1 Tie your string into an endless loop and ask a volunteer to step forward. You're going to need someone with two thumbs.

2 Pass the loop through the ring and stretch it between your volunteer's thumbs. With your right hand, pinch the string as illustrated and pull it back toward you. Hang onto it here until the trick ends. Letting go of this pinch is the last move.

3 With your left hand pinch the string as illustrated and pass it over your volunteer's thumb.

Let go, then, without any fumbling around, pinch the string again with your left hand (only this time on the other side of the ring) and bring that over to drop over your volunteer's thumb, same as before. As you go through these maneuverings, your volunteer will have to bring his hands a little closer together because you're shortening the loop a bit.

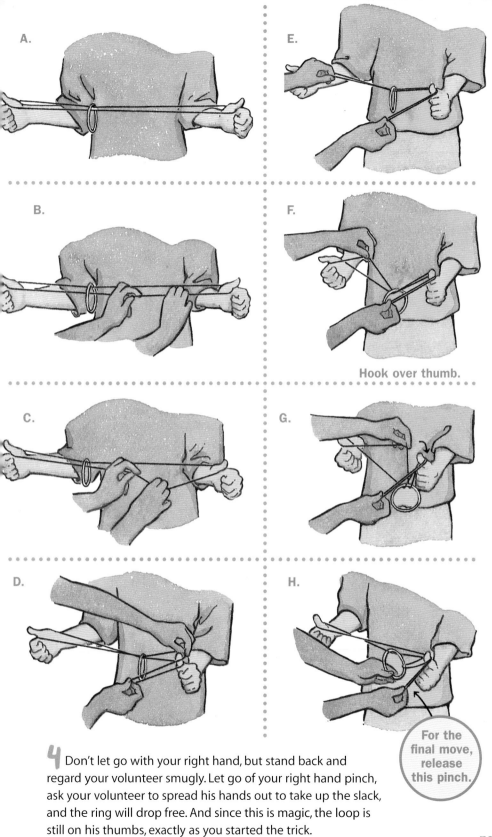

A.

B.

C.

D.

E.

F.

Hook over thumb.

G.

H.

For the final move, release this pinch.

4 Don't let go with your right hand, but stand back and regard your volunteer smugly. Let go of your right hand pinch, ask your volunteer to spread his hands out to take up the slack, and the ring will drop free. And since this is magic, the loop is still on his thumbs, exactly as you started the trick.

Spinning Ring Release

Here's how this one looks. The magician puts the steel ring onto the string. Both ends of the string are held in full view. The magician then pulls the ring off. Simple, clean, impossible.

1 Recruit a volunteer to hold one end of your string. Since that's the entire extent of his job, you don't need to be too picky about who you choose.

2 Put the ring on the string and stretch it between the two of you. Say something startling like... "Behold, one ring on string." Make a big point of the fact that the ring is ON the string... no way can you get it off.

3 Now, keeping hold of the string with one hand, grab the ring at its bottom and turn it once toward you. The string will wrap itself once around the ring. Then hold the ring as illustrated. Announce that you have locked the ring on.

Grab at the red dot...

...and twist once.

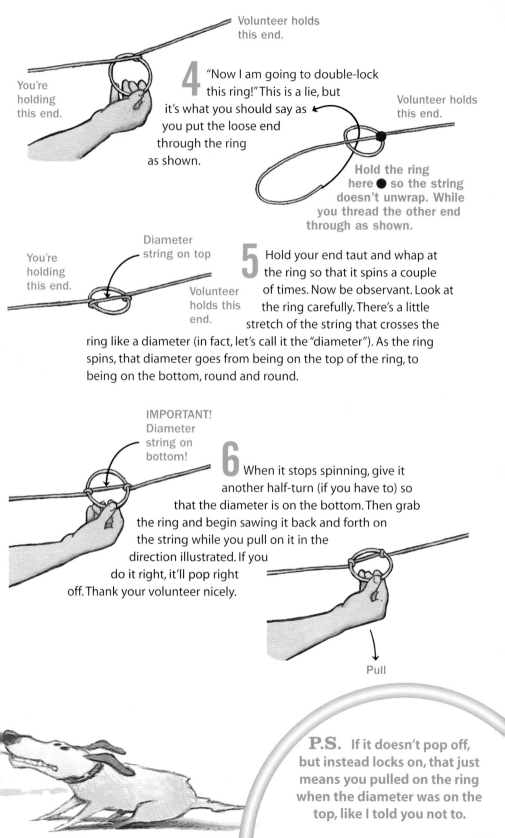

Volunteer holds this end.

You're holding this end.

4 "Now I am going to double-lock this ring!" This is a lie, but it's what you should say as you put the loose end through the ring as shown.

Volunteer holds this end.

Hold the ring here ● so the string doesn't unwrap. While you thread the other end through as shown.

You're holding this end.

Diameter string on top

Volunteer holds this end.

5 Hold your end taut and whap at the ring so that it spins a couple of times. Now be observant. Look at the ring carefully. There's a little stretch of the string that crosses the ring like a diameter (in fact, let's call it the "diameter"). As the ring spins, that diameter goes from being on the top of the ring, to being on the bottom, round and round.

IMPORTANT! Diameter string on bottom!

6 When it stops spinning, give it another half-turn (if you have to) so that the diameter is on the bottom. Then grab the ring and begin sawing it back and forth on the string while you pull on it in the direction illustrated. If you do it right, it'll pop right off. Thank your volunteer nicely.

Pull

P.S. If it doesn't pop off, but instead locks on, that just means you pulled on the ring when the diameter was on the top, like I told you not to.

RING FLIP

The quickest string and ring trick of all. Very fast, very nice. Because it's over and done in seconds, it can make a good finale.

1 Hang the loop from your hand as illustrated. Make it as wide a loop as possible.

2 Thread the bottom of the loop through the ring and bring the ring up about two-thirds of the way to your hand. Hold the ring exactly as illustrated. What happens next is, I believe, impossible to describe, but…

3 Throw the ring down hard toward the bottom of the loop. As you throw, flip the ring toward the string. This makes almost no sense, so quit reading and look at the illustrations.

4 At first, nothing will happen except that your ring will bounce off the floor. But with a little practice, and just the right combination of throw and flip, you'll be able to catch the ring onto the string in a knot (technically, "the girth hitch").

5 Once the ring is caught in this knot, you can drop one end of the string and hold it up for one and all. The whole thing takes nothing but a couple of seconds and, to your spectators, looks completely unbelievable.

With practice, you can do this 9 out of 10 times. Believe us.

THE LIKO PANG PENETRATION

This is a move variously credited to two modern magicians, Liko Pang, a Hawaiian performer, and Eric DeCamps, a New York magician. It is serious, performer quality magic. It probably requires as much practice as any single move in this book. I practiced it for hours and tried it in front of at least 15 people before I finally started fooling anybody. The good news though is that it is truly a great illusion — among the best of any in close-up magic. I suggest you work at this one. It's worth the effort.

1 The first step is simply introduction. Hand a volunteer the ring, stretch the cord between your two hands, and ask him or her to forcibly penetrate the cord with the ring, using mental powers if necessary.

2 Now take back the ring and explain that you'd like to try yourself. Locate the middle of the cord and drape it over your hand as illustrated. Move quickly through this part, giving the impression that this is all just "set-up."

3 This next move is the whole trick and will require the aforementioned hours of practice. (For nearly a week, I carried my ring and cord around with me in my pocket pulling them out and practicing at odd moments.)

4 Hold the ring exactly as illustrated, position your fingers precisely. The tip of your ring finger has to be on the ring. When you begin pushing the cord down with the ring (that's what you're going to do in a second) use the tip of your ring finger to keep the cord from sliding around.

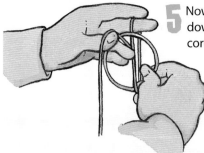

5 Now, gently, confidently, quickly, bring the ring down and begin pushing the cord with it. The cord should hit the ring right at the tip of your ring finger. That way the cord won't slide off. (From here on, when I talk about fingers, I'm talking about the fingers on the hand that's holding the cord — not the ring.)

6 Here's the true dirty work. It should take no more than a half-second. Since it is largely exposed, you have to be quick and very, very smooth. Just as you're moving the ring down, reach through it with your ring finger and snag the cord as illustrated. Your ring finger is the only finger that has to move. Keep moving the ring down — don't change the rhythm — and talk about anything but what you are doing.

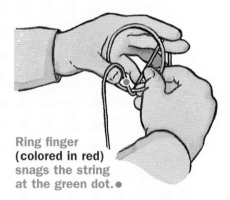

Ring finger **(colored in red)** snags the string at the green dot.●

It'll take a couple hours of practice before this move looks smooth.

Ring finger has the string.

7 As you continue to move the ring down, use your thumb to re-catch the string that your ring finger snagged. (The illustrations make much more sense than these instructions.)

With practice, you can do these two finger moves so quickly that they're nearly invisible.

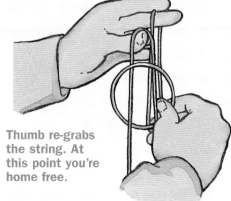

Thumb re-grabs the string. At this point you're home free.

Trick continues ☞

YOUR VIEW

THE AUDIENCE'S VIEW

8 Hold the string taut with the ring. Again, keep the cord up against the tip of your ring finger, otherwise it will slide.

Keep the cord up against the tip of your ring finger.

How to MAGIC

9 Hold the ring quite still. The "introductory moves" are over and now you are about to perform. The spectators are staring at the ring and unless they have X-ray vision, they're looking at a ring pressed against the bottom of a loop. But the ring is clearly not on the cord. Not yet.

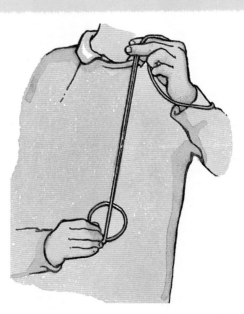

10 Talk for a moment about what you are going to try to do — momentarily melt a small gap into the ring so as to permit the passage of the string. The ring will jump onto the string and the gap will instantly re-seal itself. Explain that this may sound easy, but in fact it is no mean task.

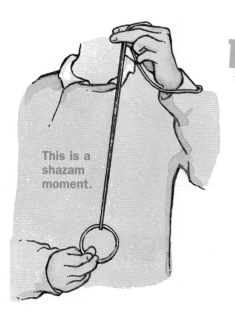

This is a shazam moment.

11 When you've rambled on for a moment or two about this, stop talking. Draw all their attention to the ring. You want this to happen right in front of their eyes. Then suddenly tweak the ring and jerk it down. The ring will apparently jump onto the string. Check the illustrations again.

Shazam!

It's a fabulous illusion and you should milk it for everything you can. If you're doing a number of string and ring tricks, I'd save this as your clincher.

A simple trick but with a very good effect. All you need is a rubber band and a large ring (a graduation ring is perfect).

The Rubber Band
IMPOSSIBILITY

1 Pass the ring and rubber band around for inspection. Both are completely normal.

2 Hold the ring and rubber band as illustrated. Practice this next move a few times before you go public with it. The idea is to pinch the rubber band inside the ring in a quicker-than-the-eye move. (If you're not that smooth, just do it under the table where nobody can see).

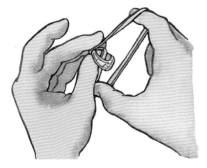

Move the ring up and down.

3 Now hold the ring and band as illustrated and move the ring up and down, slowly. You are actually just stretching the rubber band, but it looks as if the band has penetrated the ring and you are moving the ring on the band. If you do it right, this stands up to some pretty close inspection. But if someone starts to get too close, you can cover the ring for a moment with your hand, release the pinch, and suddenly, everything's back to normal.

This ring is <u>not</u> on the rubber band. But it should look like it is.

Nutty ⬡ String

Another good piece of close-up magic with a long and
distinguished career. All you'll need is a volunteer,
a hankie or bandana, your string and two large
identical ⬡ ⬡ — the bigger the better.

1 Put the two nuts in your pocket
along with your hankie. Hand your
string to your volunteer and ask that
she examine it in every detail. Then
hand her one of the nuts and ask that
she do the same. ("Fascinating, isn't it?")

2 Now carefully, slowly, in full
view, thread the string through
the nut and hand both ends over to
your volunteer. ("Hold on to these with
everything you've got!") Display and
describe the situation in tedious detail.

Behold!
The nut is
in place.

("**Observe. This string is held irrevocably
in the hands of this well-muscled
volunteer. The nut is threaded
irrevocably onto the string.
There is nothing funny
about the string, nothing
funny about the nut, and
nothing funny about me.
NO WAY CAN I GET THIS
THING OFF!! Right?**")

Trick continues ☞

3 The story continues:

"Now, to make this even harder, I am going to blindfold…
this nut!" Reach into your pocket and pull out the hankie and
(discreetly) the duplicate nut. Cover the nut (the one on the
string) with your hankie and reach underneath with both
hands (one of them concealing the duplicate). This is the part
that takes a little practice. Ask for a bit of slack and pull an inch
or two of the string through the hole in your duplicate nut.
Enough to hold it on.

**The duplicate gets
attached like this.**

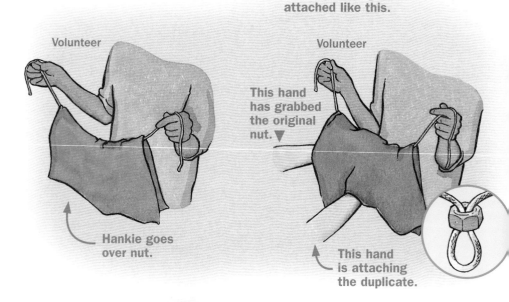

Volunteer

Volunteer

**This hand
has grabbed
the original
nut. ▼**

**Hankie goes
over nut.**

**This hand
is attaching
the duplicate.**

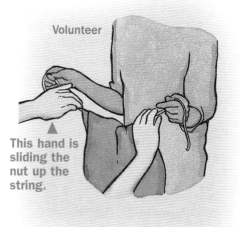

Volunteer

**This hand is
sliding the
nut up the
string.**

4 Then, cover the original
nut with your hand and
begin sliding both hands away
from the duplicate, up the string,
out from under the hankie and
up toward your volunteer's
well-muscled hands. Make the
following request in hushed
tones: **"Now let me have the
string while you, slowly,
remove the hankie."**

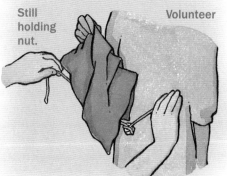

Volunteer removes hankie.

Still holding nut.

Volunteer

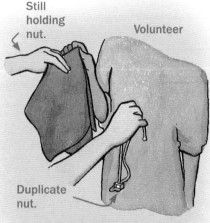

Still holding nut.

Volunteer

Duplicate nut.

Volunteer returns hankie to you while you return the string.

5 The hankie is then removed while you hold the ends of the string for a moment. Your volunteer is left to look at the duplicate nut which is attached in some funny way to the string. They suspect something, but they're not sure what. Now, ask them to give you the hankie so you can give them back the ends of the string.

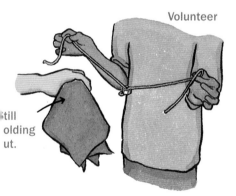

Volunteer

Still olding ut.

Ditch nut and hankie.

6 This is a really filthy move, so practice it. Take the hankie back with the guilty hand. Simply slide it (and the nut) off the end of the string, as you hand the string over and take back the hankie. Then ditch both nut and hankie in your pocket, or anywhere. Make this whole maneuver casual and incidental-seeming. Your volunteer should still be focussed on the nut in the middle of the string.

7 Give the following climactic instructions as you cup your empty hands under the nut: **"Please use as much care as possible as you tighten this string. Magic is a very sensitive art."** As they do that, the nut will drop off in your hands.

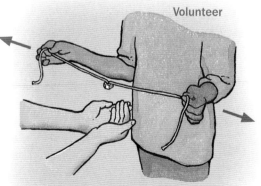

Volunteer

Volunteer pulls string, nut falls off.

8 Say thank you.

Among the thousands of magic tricks, only a very few are so simple, clean and effective that they deserve the term "elegant." This, I believe, is one of them.

The Ring Slide

1 You'll need a finger ring and a length of rope. Say about three or four feet.

2 Thread the ring onto the rope and hold as pictured, palm open and up. Stand up and gather everyone around to look at this. You have nothing to hide.

Ring on string.

Perform the next two steps promptly and efficiently. It's the "introduction," so move quickly and say something that sounds introduction-like.

3 Close your fingers over the rope and ring and turn your hand palm down. Now secretly work the ring into position so that you are barely hanging onto it. See the illustration for the idea. To drop it (so that it slides down the rope), all you need to do is relax your fingers a tiny fraction. To keep this tenuous grip invisible, hold your hands kind of low. Waist height is about right.

Right hand

Ring is barely held. →

Bottom view

4 Now for the only move. Since this is still the "introduction" do it quickly. Take the dangling ends of the rope and cross them over the back of your hand exactly as illustrated.

Ring is here.

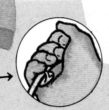

Take the rope end with the red dot. ●

Cross it over the back of your hand.

◀ LET ALL OF THE ROPE RUN THROUGH THIS HAND.

Ring

THIS IS THE DIRTY MOVE.

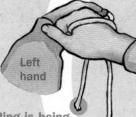

Left hand

Right hand

Repeat the move with the other dangling end, the blue dot. As you do so, secretly drop the ring into the moving hand. Do this quickly, confidently, smoothly.

Conceal the ring in your hand and slide it entirely off the rope as you finish the cross over.

Ring is being switched from one hand to the other now.

Trick continues ☞

5 Now that the ring is out of your rope-hand, the dirty work is over and you can start the fun. Explain that you've now set the scene and are ready to perform. Have a volunteer (or volunteers) hold both ends of the rope while you keep a grip on the middle. Tell the volunteers to stretch the rope taut. Then, open your hand very slowly. Where'd the ring go?

That's easy, you dropped it into your back pocket, or onto the rug behind you while everybody was watching all the shenanigans going on with the volunteers.

I love this little piece of sleight. It's small, simple and very clean. Practice it for a couple of minutes in front of a mirror. In order to ensure invisibility, remember to keep your hands sort of low, about waist height.

Ring

Ring on rope and in hand. Slide off the rope. Dirty work done.

The ability to draw your spectators' attention away from any dirty work is called "misdirection" and it lies very close to the black heart of magic.

Some professional performers who are superb at this one skill never even bother to develop particularly good dexterity.

If no one is even watching the guilty hand, why bother with a lot of practice? This wonderful little trick relies on misdirection almost completely.

RING ZING

1 Gather together your string and trusty ring. In one hand, hold the two of them **exactly as illustrated.** The string should be clipped between your ring and middle fingers three or four inches from one end. The rest hangs free. Your audience sees and knows that the ring is off the string.

2 Here comes the only move. It will be a couple of hours of lonesome practice in front of a mirror before you'll fool a soul with it, but it's the one and only move you'll need.

Trick continues ☞

3 With your empty hand, grab the string as high as you can and run it through your fingers till you get to a few inches from the end. Stop and hang on. Although only one hand does the grabbing, the whole pulling motion should be done with both hands. Both arms in fact. It has to be very big, very smooth, and very natural. Why? Because it's covering the dirty work.

Move this hand **up.**

Empty hand grabs and slides down the rope.

◀ ...while the dirty move happens here. (Keep reading...)

Your audience will watch this hand...

How to do the dirty work

String is through the ring. The audience is not aware.

4 And what is the dirty work? Back to the hand that's holding the ring. As you move it in this broad pulling motion, the thumb is not idle. It should reach through the ring, snag the three or four inches that are hanging down and pull them back through. The ring is now loaded onto the string, but you have to cover that fact.

5 As soon as you stop the pulling, don't pause for an instant, bring both hands together and grab the ring exactly as illustrated. Don't fumble this part. When your hands stop moving you have to look exactly as per the illustration.

THE FINAL POSITION
(Your Point of View)

THE FINAL POSITION
(Their Point of View)

Ring still does not look as if it's on string.

From the front, if everything is precisely positioned, you've created a powerful illusion. It looks for all the world as if the ring is gripped separate and quite innocent, while the string is simply looped between your two hands. From the spectator's point of view, all you've done is grab the string and pull it through your hand. Little do they know.

6 Now you can slow everything down. Show off the arrangement of string and ring. What you are going to try and do, you should explain, is force the ring onto the bottom of this loop by "zinging" it downwards… "while at the same time imparting enough quantum rotational force to it so that the molecules of the ring are sufficiently agitated to instantaneously permit the passage of the string molecules…"

Get ready to zing the ring down.

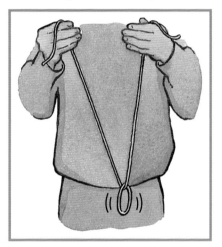

BEFORE   AFTER

7 This goes on as long as your audience can stand it. Finally, on the count of three, hang on to the string, but shoot the ring down hard. The audience will see a flash of movement, then suddenly the ring will self-arrest onto the bottom of the loop. Exactly as predicted.

Cut and Restored ROPE

Taking a piece of rope, cutting it, and then suddenly restoring it to its full length again is one of the oldest effects in magic. Amongst the many dozens of ways to perform it, the version that follows is probably the neatest.

1 You're going to need a length of soft cotton rope (clothesline), four or five feet long, and a pair of magic scissors. Announce that you are going to locate the middle of this rope.

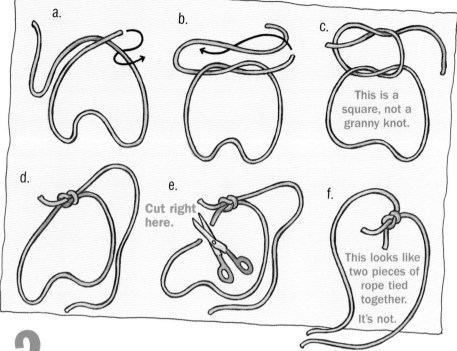

a.

b.

c.

This is a square, not a granny knot.

d.

e.

Cut right here.

f.

This looks like two pieces of rope tied together. It's not.

2 Find the middle and drape it from that point over your finger. So far, your audience is probably not too impressed.

3 Now take one end of the rope, bring it up to the middle of the rope, and tie a square knot. Follow the illustration. Don't make it tight. Just snug. And make very sure you've tied a square, not a granny.

4 Get your scissors out and cut the rope as per the illustration. Practice this part and cut exactly where indicated. If you don't cut right, embarrassing things will happen.

5 Set down your magic scissors in an obscured place, behind a book or on the floor or something.

6 Stand up on a chair and announce that you have now cut your rope in half and tied it back together! Hold it up by both ends, snap it tight and wait for the applause to die down.

Wait though! The trick's not over! For your grand finale, you will proceed to wrap the rope entirely around one hand! This is called the **Amazing One-Hand Wrap**, and it was shown to you by an ancient fakir.

Nothing tricky going on here. Yet.

A

B

C

The dirty work doesn't start until you...

D

...grab the knot...

E

...and secretly slide it off.

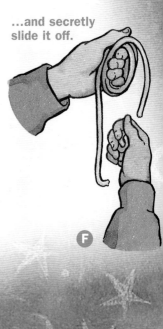

F

8 Complete the **Amazing One-Hand Wrap** promptly. Don't dwell on it. As you do so, the knot will slide off in your wrapping hand. Note that if you cut a little too long, the knot will be too big to hide in your hand and some sharp-eyed spectator will catch you red-handed. If you cut right though, it should be small and concealable.

9 Reach for your magic scissors and as you get them, ditch the little piece of rope that came off in your hand. Do this promptly and you'll never get caught.

10 Wave the scissors over your wrapped hand and ask your audience to say the magic words. Put the scissors down in a new and visible place and pull the wraps off your hand. When you've finished, you'll be holding one piece of unknotted rope. Hold it up and smile.

The Center Tear

This is a great trick. It requires just a little bit of practice off by yourself since there is one small move. But it's not hard. The key skill is lying. You have to convince everyone at the table that you can really read minds. Mumble and groan a lot. Hold your head in your hands. That kind of thing.

1 Everybody should be at the table. Have somebody provide a simple sheet of clean paper. (Half the size of a regular 8-1/2" x 11" would be ideal.) Draw an oval right in the center of it. Close your eyes and begin to mumble.

This is the center corner. The secret word is on the other side of it. Don't really mark it with an **x**. We just did that to make things clearer.

2 Hand the paper to someone and allow them to write a word (any word) in the oval. Then instruct them to fold the paper in half. Then, tell them to turn the paper 90 degrees and fold it in half again. Now open your eyes and look mysterious.

3 Ask for the paper and without a lot of fumbling around do the following:

Identify the Center Corner (see illustration) and put it in the upper right. (The center corner is where the oval is drawn. Just on the other side.) Then tear the paper down the middle. You now have two "paper packs." Put the pack with the Center Corner on top, keep the Center Corner in the upper right, turn 90 degrees and tear both "packs" again right down the middle.

Keep your eye on the center corner.

Tear here

Secret word

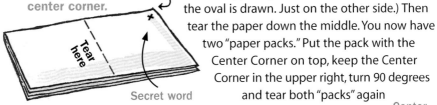

Stack the halves, then turn to get this.

Tear here

Center corner

Secret word

Make a final stack, but keep the center corner on top.

4 Now for the only move. Practice this part well. Hold the paper pack in front of you, and ask that your audience believe in you very deeply. Announce that you would like a volunteer for this part. ("It doesn't hurt… much. Any hands?")

5 While everyone looks around for the volunteer, steal the top slip off the pack as you lay the rest on the table.

The top slip is the one with the center corner. If you've folded and torn correctly, it will contain the word. Look at the illustrations for the steal move. It's not hard, but practice a bit.

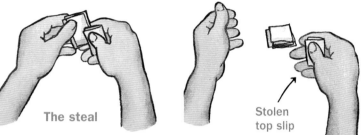

The steal

Stolen top slip

6 Ask your volunteer to chew on the paper. **("It helps me concentrate.")** As they consider that, put the stolen slip on your lap. If they're a little squeamish about chewing, have them tear and crumple as much as possible. While they're doing that, reach down and unfold the paper. Then, drop into a deep trance, lean back, look down (hands at your temples), and read the word off your lap.

7 Now for the fun. Start guessing. The word is "dog?" A scene will begin to form in your mind. You might describe it thusly: "I see… a… small animal. Ugly little thing. Five legs… no… four. Furry. IT'S A RABBIT!! No, that's not right… it's chasing the mailman… IT'S A HAMSTER… No, that's not right…" You get the idea. Drag it on as long as you like.

The Flip and Flop Force

In the magic biz, a "card force" is any maneuver that forces the spectator to pick a card which the magician has already pre-selected. ("Pick a card! Pick a pre-selected card!") Once the spectator has "randomly" selected a card which he thinks is a secret known only to him, then lots of fun things are possible. The following maneuver is a neat little card force. Use it by itself for a magic quickie, or add it to one of the two tricks that follow this for a full-on Magic Routine.

1 Take a regular deck of cards and shuffle through them, noting the top card. (To note the top card, just turn the deck over and riffle through it. Brazen, but it works every time.)

Start here. You know what the top card is.

Let's say the top card is the ace of spades. Hand the deck to your spectator and ask him to lift a bunch of cards off the top and hold them separately. Any number he wants. Free choice. (If necessary, you can demonstrate this once, then re-shuffle, note the top card, and start over.)

Cut a packet off the top...

2 Now ask him to take that top packet of cards he's just cut, flip it over so that it's face up, and put it back on top of the deck.

...flip it over...

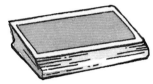

...and replace it on top.

**Cut again,
deeper...**

3 Now ("Just to doubly randomize all this...")
ask him to do it again with the following
instructions: "Cut the deck again, only deeper
than last time. Take that packet of cut cards,
turn them over, face up, and replace them
on top of the deck."

Key Point: Make sure
he cuts the deck deeper
on the second go-round.

**Face-up
top cards**

**...flip and replace
on top...**

4 Now the deck is sitting there, a bunch of cards
are face up, on top. Just for the record, recap
what has just happened.

**"Here's our deck. You've cut it not
just once, but twice. Both times,
randomly. But let's mix it up even more.
Throw away all those cards that are face
up. We won't even use them."**

**...then throw off
the face up cards.**

5 After he's done that, ask him to carefully remove
the top card from what's left of the deck and hold
it close to his chest. This is his Secret Card.
He should reveal it to no one.

He doesn't have to. It's the ace of spades, the
card that was at the top at the beginning.

**The first card face down
should be the old top card.**

6
From here
in, it's all
up to you.
You can fall into a
deep hypnotic trance and
reveal the card in a voice
from a previous lifetime, or
(my recommendation) you
can tell him to hang onto
that card and go into either
the Spook Writing trick,
or The Fruit Card Trick.
Keep reading.

SPOOK WRITING

This is another piece of "component magic."
It can be done by itself as a quickie, but, if you put it together
with the Flip and Flop Force, the two of them deliver a fabulous
one-two punch that'll leave them reeling. All the props you'll
need are business cards and a rubber band. If business cards
aren't around, you can use a deck of playing cards,
or standard 3"x5" cards instead.

1 First, a bit of preparation. Business cards are the best, so if you have them, put about 25 together with a rubber band. If you have to use 3x5 cards instead, cut them very neatly in half so they look about the size of the cards in the illustrations. A last resort is a deck of playing cards. But whatever you're using, wrap them together with a medium-width rubber band.

2 Still out of view of the audience, take off the top card and write a few magic words on the card underneath. What you choose to write depends on whether you are doing this as part of a larger trick, or all by itself. For the purpose of this explanation, let's say you're doing this as part of the **Flip and Flop Force**. In that case, write the words "ace of spades" on the card.

3 Don't write all over the card; make sure you stay to one side or the other of the rubber band. On the other half of the rubber band, in a corner of the same card, mark an "X." Incidentally, if you're using business cards, you'll be writing on the unprinted side; if you're using playing cards, write on the backs.

Cover your magic words with a half-card.

4 Now, cut the first card you pulled precisely in half. Toss one half away and fit the other over your magic words. Shift the rubber band around until it covers the cut mark exactly. Make sure it's a good and snug rubber band. The best kind to use are the medium-sized bands. The big fat ones look a little suspicious. The little tiny ones don't cover well enough.

A half-card sits on top of a full card. Cover the edge with a rubber band.

5 When you're done, you'll have a normal-appearing pack of cards, wrapped with a rubber band around the middle and with an "X" appearing in one corner of the top card. (Actually, it's a half-card sitting on top of a full card.)

6 Time for the audience. Line them up by I.Q. and don't pick the first one. After you've made your choice, hand your volunteer the deck of cards and explain that you will need a signature.

"If you could sign the card at the X?"

Finished product. Signature in place.

Trick continues☞

7 Here's the one and only move. As you take back the deck, admire the signature for a moment, display it to one and all and then pull it out of the deck as you flip the deck over. It's very simple, very natural. The act of turning the deck over covers the fact that there's a half-card still left on top. Toss the pack aside.

The cut-in-half card stays.

The signature card is pulled out.

8 If you were just doing this trick by itself, all you'd need to do now is hand the card back to your volunteer where he could suddenly discover that the words "I.O.U. $1 million" (or some such) have appeared above his signature. But, since that's not the version we're describing, here's what you do.

9 Keep the card. Keep it written side down and place it on top of your head (if you think you can keep it there. Otherwise, right on the table will do).

10 Jump right into the **Flip and Flop Force** (page 78). Just make sure that the ace of spades is the card on top, the one your volunteer finally ends up with.

11 At the conclusion to the Force, when your volunteer is clutching his secret card, known only to him, take the signed business card off your head (or off the table) and without turning it over, give it to him and ask him to rub it against his secret card, and then, in what has to be one of the more devastating finishes in close-up magic, ask him to slowly turn both over. (**"That is your signature, isn't it?"**)

THE

FRUIT

CARD TRICK

This is the Big Trick of this book. In fact, it's so big, it requires two other tricks in the middle — the Flip and Flop Force and the Gypsy Switch. Not only that, you'll need to put in a few minutes of unusual preparation before your audience arrives. But it's all worth it. The effect is one hundred percent outrageous. This is going to be your show-stopper.

1 These are the props you'll need: a deck of cards with an extra (identical) ace of spades, a hankie and an orange. Plus, you should write (in big letters) on a 3"x5" card the mysterious words, "Look in the orange." Then tear it up into eight pieces exactly, paper clip them together and pocket them.

2 Here's your preparation: Shuffle through your deck and put the ace of spades on top. Set the deck aside. Then take your duplicate ace of spades and tear one corner of it off. Put the corner in a fold of your clothes, tucked in behind your belt, in your cuff… someplace you'll be able to retrieve it discreetly. Take what's left of the card and roll it into a tube. Now you have to get that tube into the middle of an orange. (I'm serious.) Cut a tiny piece out of the end of your orange and don't lose it. Look at the illustrations for the idea. You want to make this an invisible cut.

Roll your ace into a tight tube.

Trick continues ☞

Putting the rolled-up ace into the orange.

3 Push your rolled-up ace of spades into the middle of the orange and replace the top. (Some perfectionists have even been known to glue it back on). When you're done, the orange should look untouched. Then put your customized piece of fruit somewhere you'll remember. Maybe you have a bowl of fruit handy? Or you could put it in the refrigerator? Or just stick it down your pants.

Anyway, bring on your audience. You're ready.

4 Explain that you have no idea what you're doing, but this is how you think it should go. Produce the deck of cards. Fumble with it for a moment, you could shuffle it, or even drop it… just make sure that when you're done, the top card is still the ace of spades.

5 Now go through the **Flip and Flop Force** (page 78) with a suitable volunteer. Practice this well. It can help if you look as if you don't know what you're doing, but just make sure that's an act. At the finish, your volunteer should be holding his Secret Card, the ace of spades, revealing it to no one. **One more point:** At some point in all this, at an opportune moment, retrieve the torn corner from your clothing unnoticed and palm it in your left hand.

6 **Now it starts to get serious.** Ask that your volunteer tear his card into fourths (only fourths!) and hand the four pieces over to you. Make sure he keeps the card and the pieces face down. **("I don't want to see your card!")** Take the pieces in your right hand and tear the whole pack in half again. Meanwhile, your left hand is palming the corner that you tore off your duplicate ace of spades. Put the eight pieces of torn card into your left hand, on top of your palmed piece and set all nine pieces down onto the table.

7 Bring a paper clip out of your pocket and as you start to clip the pieces together, take the new piece, the one you added (it should be on the bottom), out of the pack and hand it back over to your volunteer. **("Here, let me give you a receipt.")** This is a beautiful move. It's so dirty, and yet, it's so completely invisible. Make sure that during all of this, you keep the card down so that neither you nor any audience member sees what card has been torn.

The "receipt"

8 Now you have to get rid of the eight pieces of card you've got in your hand. Most magicians, when they're faced with the need to vanish something do it with the help of a gimmicked prop. A phony envelope, or a lined bag or something similar. But they're not really necessary. If you have a very smooth French Drop, you could employ that to vanish the pieces, but I really think the Gypsy Switch is your best option. It's quick, clean and convincing.

9 Put the clipped cards down on the table and go into both pockets with your hands. In one hand, you should come up with your hankie; in the other, palm the clipped-together pack of 3x5 cards you prepared at the beginning. Practice this palm. **Keep it natural. This trick is too good to blow it here.**

10 Run through the Gypsy Switch exactly as described on page 42. Do it quickly since you don't want your audience to forget the main plot of the real trick. When you're done, your volunteer should be holding a hankie with the 3x5 cards wrapped into it.

(Of course, that's not what he thinks he's holding. He thinks he's holding a hankie with the torn-up pieces of his ace of spades.) You, meanwhile, can pocket or put into your lap the real cards at an opportune moment. Ask your volunteer to treasure that hankie, but not to open it yet.

11 Once you've ditched the torn-up cards, you are over the only hurdle this trick presents in terms of physical handling. **Now for the real fun.**

12 Lower your voice. "Blow on your hankie very gently. If you have any magic in you at all, your Secret Card will be fully restored." When he opens the hankie up, after he gets over his disappointment, ask that he try to put the torn-up 3x5 card back together. ("Why not? It seems like the least you can do…")

13 From here on, it only gets better. When he's finally gotten his torn-up message back together, and as he's looking around for an orange, just stand up and let your customized orange fall down onto the ground (or go to the fridge, or over to your bowl of fruit…) Then, wordlessly, hand it over. When he peels off the skin and extracts the soggy, rolled up Secret Card, act as surprised as anyone else, then suggest that it be matched against the receipt. When the torn corner fits perfectly, just shrug your shoulders.

("What can I say?")

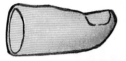

THUMB TIP POINTERS

The little plastic thumb that accompanies this book is called a thumb tip and it has one of the longest, most distinguished careers of any prop in magic. Long before rabbits and top hats were on the scene, magicians were employing thumb tips (actually just metal thimbles) to vanish objects into thin air. A well-used thumb tip creates absolutely impossible effects. A scarf is pushed into a clenched fist, the fist is opened to reveal an empty hand. A small glass of water or a shakerful of salt is treated the same way. Again, the fist is opened, nothing is there. Clean, simple and completely baffling.

Slip the thumb tip onto your thumb and your first impression will undoubtedly be a sense of deep skepticism. ("A blind man in the back of the auditorium could see this thing.") Hold your hand wrong, wave your thumb around, and you'd be right. You'll be sticking up the proverbial sore thumb. But now take a spectator's point of view. Step in front of a mirror, point your thumb tip directly at it, and suddenly things aren't quite so obvious. Then curl your fingers in such a way as to completely conceal the tip with your other fingers. A few moments in front of a mirror and you should realize two things: One, the thumb is a pretty easy finger to keep out of sight and two, that's what you're going to have to do to get away with it. As you practice keeping your thumb in a low profile mode, remember that the true pros could use one painted fluorescent orange and still get away with it.

Following are the key things to keep in mind:

Practice in front of a mirror so that you can keep the spectator's point of view.

Keep the thumb tip hand (the "guilty" hand) moving when it is not held at your side, and keep the thumb behind the other fingers.

When you need to demonstrate that your hand is empty, always point directly at your audience (briefly) and say something appropriate like "Let me show you how this works..."

Practice looking as if you've never practiced.

One last point. For a beginner, the thumb tip takes a frightening amount of gall to use since the risks are so high. Produce a scarf from a dollar bill, get away with it, and you're a living miracle. But let someone spot the thumb tip you did it with, and you're a dead duck. It's a high-risk game and a scary height to fall from. Fortunately, I have a couple of suggestions that might help.

1 If you're a little embarrassed by the sheer fraudulence of the thumb tip, don't worry, that's a common problem with many beginners. It's called the "honesty" hang-up, and you'll get over it. Don't begin your career with thumb tip tricks. Start with small, hard-to-muff tricks and accompany them with little tiny fibs. Then slowly work up to harder tricks

and horrendous lies. (Thumb tip tricks, incidentally, count as medium-hard tricks requiring horrendous lies.)

2 When you think you're ready to go public with a thumb tip, start with very short audiences — say 10 years old and under. You'd be amazed at what you can get away with.

3 Incidentally, the color of this thumb tip can be customized to your own skin tone if you choose to do so. Use a permanent marker pen for the job, but remember, with good technique, the thumb can be fluorescent lime and no one will catch you.

The Vanishing Scarf

You can't call yourself a REAL magician until you can make a scarf vanish and reappear. This is Basic Magic 101.

1 Before anyone is watching, slip your thumb tip onto your thumb loosely. (Use whichever hand is most comfortable for you. For the purposes of explanation, whichever hand has the tip on is the "guilty" hand.) Then use it to hold your scarf. If you hold it right, the thumb tip will be concealed behind the scarf. (If you don't hold it right, someone in your audience is liable to wonder why your thumb looks twice as big as normal.)

2 Explain to your audience that you're going to paint this scarf "air-colored." As you're going on like this, absently run the scarf through your hand as illustrated — ditching the tip into your fist. **This is a key move. Practice it well.**

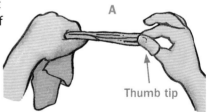

A

Thumb tip

B

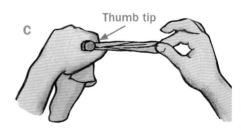

C

Thumb tip

3 Flap the scarf around for a moment for effect, and then begin tucking it into your clenched fist containing the tip. Explain that you are now dunking the tip into air-colored paint.

Do a final push with your thumb slipping on the tip. Now pay attention to the next move. It's important.

4 Keep your clenched fist closed. Use your guilty hand to point briefly at your audience, showing them the end of the tip. Since that hand is obviously empty, drop it to your side with the fingers held naturally in such a way as to obscure the tip. Practice this so it looks as if you've never practiced it.

5 Hold your clenched fist up and peek into it. Dwell on this part since it's your punch line. Talk about air-colored paint in general, how hard it is to find, etc. Then slowly open your fist, finger by finger. **("There you have it, one air-colored scarf.")**

Thumb tip filled with scarf is in this fist.

6 Time now for a little mime. Pinch the invisible "scarf" between thumb and forefinger. Toss it around, grab it, blow on it to keep it up, finally end up with the invisible card in your guilty hand. Then, to reappear it, just pantomime the same move you began the trick with — stroke the "scarf" through your innocent hand leaving off the loaded tip. **Key move again, so practice.**

7 The rest is all show. You can peer into your fist, "spit" into it to wash off the paint, mumble ancient spells, then slowly pull the scarf out. Wave it around to distract everyone while you plug your thumb back into the tip. (This is a one-hand move since you're using the thumb that's on the same hand that's holding the tip.) Then, to finish off, take the scarf back with your guilty hand and stuff it (and tip) into a pocket.

Finis.

Silken Dollar

Another chapter in Magic 101.
Producing a scarf out of a dollar bill is a magic classic.
A simple, completely impossible effect. You'll need
your thumb tip and a crisp piece of legal tender.

1. Begin the trick by sticking both hands into your pockets, searching for a dollar bill. The bill should be in one pocket, the thumb tip (already packed with scarf) should be in the other. With one hand, slip on the thumb tip, with the other, grab the bill. Bring both hands up to display your riches in the manner illustrated.

You can keep the tip undetected by obeying

The Three Laws of Thumb Tips

1. Keep the guilty hand moving naturally and confidently.

2. From the audience's point of view, when the tip is sideways, it's pretty obvious. End on, though, it is very nearly invisible.

3. You should use the four other fingers or the bill to obscure the thumb. But don't look cramped or awkward.

2. Flip the dollar over once or twice, then begin wrapping the tip with the bill as you slip it off. As with any guilty move, do it smoothly and confidently. (And you might mention that dollar bills are printed on special paper with threads of fabric woven into it. Makes counterfeiting more difficult. If you look carefully at a bill, you can see the fabric...)

Look at the illustrations to see what happens next.

SILK FROM A DOLLAR

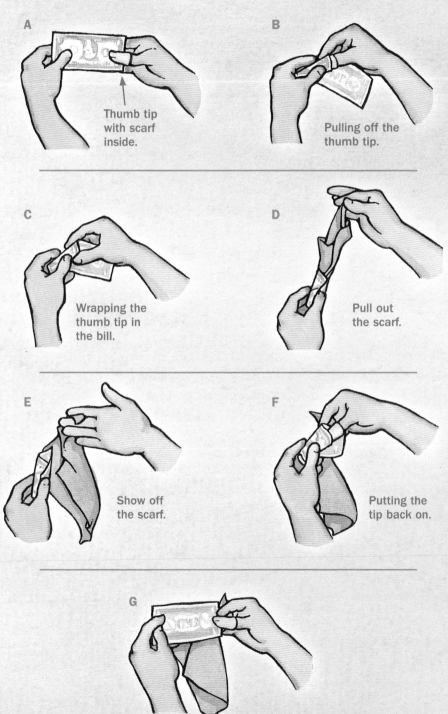

A Thumb tip with scarf inside.

B Pulling off the thumb tip.

C Wrapping the thumb tip in the bill.

D Pull out the scarf.

E Show off the scarf.

F Putting the tip back on.

G

Trick continues ☞

As with all magic, the way to practice this trick is to review reality. Do as many of the moves as you can without the thumb tip, preferably in front of a mirror. Study the natural look, then try to imitate it exactly. Remember, in this trick (like most), let reality be your guide.

HOW TO PUT THE SILK BACK IN THE DOLLAR

After the scarf is out, slip on the thumb tip, pinch bill and scarf between forefinger and thumb tip, wave both hands openly (fingers and thumb tip pointed directly at your audience). They can see your hands are obviously empty. Then put the bill and scarf back into your pocket and ditch the tip. You're clean.

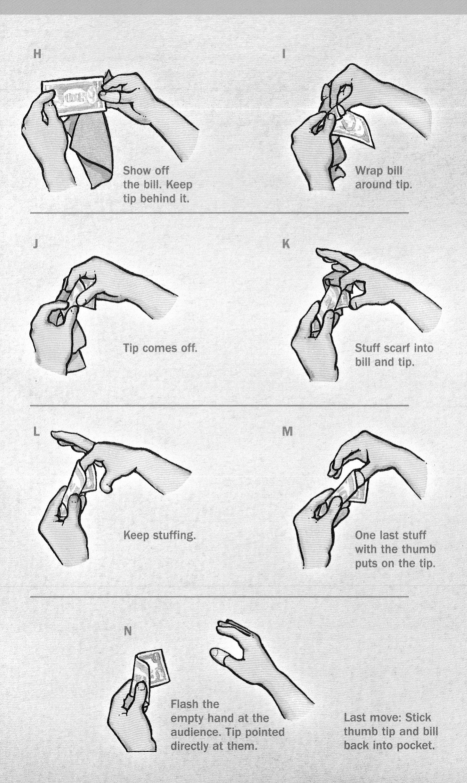

H

Show off the bill. Keep tip behind it.

I

Wrap bill around tip.

J

Tip comes off.

K

Stuff scarf into bill and tip.

L

Keep stuffing.

M

One last stuff with the thumb puts on the tip.

N

Flash the empty hand at the audience. Tip pointed directly at them.

Last move: Stick thumb tip and bill back into pocket.

Cut and Restored Ribbon

A classic thumb-tip trick. Simple to do, but a completely confounding effect. You'll need a bit of tape, a pair of scissors, a few feet of ribbon and your thumb tip.

1 First, a bit of preparation. Cut off about two inches of ribbon, fold it into a loop, and tape the ends of it inside the tip. It's a little awkward doing the taping since you're working in close quarters, but it's possible. When you're finished, the loop should pop up out of the tip. Stick the rest of the ribbon in one pocket and the prepared thumb tip in the other. Bring on the crowd.

2 Reach both hands into your pockets looking for your ribbon. With one hand, pull out the ribbon, with the other, slip on your thumb tip. Drop the thumb tip hand (the guilty one) to your side with the tip obscured by your fingers. Your other hand should be the main attraction. Flash the ribbon around and talk it up. (**"Look at this incredible ribbon! What's so special about it? For one thing, it's all in one piece…"**)

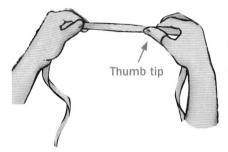

Thumb tip

3 Now stretch a section of the ribbon between your hands. A natural grab will obscure the thumb tip.

4 Next, fold the ribbon in half and hold it in your left hand. Key point: None of the ribbon should appear above your left hand, all below. Then, with your guilty hand reach into your left fist to pull the ribbon into view. As you do this, slip off the tip and pull out the prepared loop. This move has got to be practiced and smooth. Any fumbling around here and you could be in trouble.

Thumb tip

Thumb tip in fist

Pulling out the little piece of ribbon that's taped in the tip.

Trick continues ☞

5 Extract the little loop and whip out your scissors. Cut the loop cleanly in half, display your destructive handiwork and then tuck the cut ends back into your hand (your thumb tip, actually). Make the final tuck with your thumb (slipping on the tip). Don't let go of the ribbon with your left, but reach down with your guilty hand for the tail end.

Put thumb tip back on.

6 Grab the ribbon so as to obscure the tip and then slowly pull it out of your left hand — which gradually opens revealing one complete, uncut ribbon. Clean, simple, incredible.

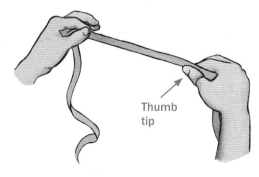

Thumb tip

CAN'T GET ENOUGH?

Here are some simple ways to keep the Klutz coming.

KLUTZ.com
Come on in!
OPEN 24 HOURS

1. Order more of the supplies that came with this book at **klutz.com**. It's quick, it's easy and, seriously, where else are you going to find this exact stuff?

2. Get your hands on a copy of The Klutz Catalog. To request a free copy of our mail order catalog, go to **klutz.com/catalog**.

3. Become a **Klutz Insider** and get e-mail about new releases, special offers, contests, games, goofiness and who-knows-what-all. If you're a grown-up who wants to receive e-mail from Klutz, head to **klutz.com/certified**.

If any of this sounds good to you, but you don't feel like going online right now, just give us a call at **1-800-737-4123**. We'd love to hear from you.

More Great Books
from Klutz

If you enjoyed *The Klutz Book of Magic* and would like to become
even more amazing, check out the Klutz books
Magnetic Magic and *Coin Magic*.

Battery Science

**Building Cards™
How to Build Castles**

**Building Cards™
How to Build Spaceships**

Capsters™

**The Best Card Games
in the Galaxy**

The Footbag Book

**Juggling for the
Complete Klutz®**

**The Klutz Book
of Knots**

Origami

**Potholders and
Other Loopy Projects**

Stop the Watch®

The Solar Car Book

The Spiral Draw Book

**Tricky Pix: Do-It-Yourself
Trick Photography**

The Klutz Yo-Yo Book

**Design, Art Direction
and Production**
Kate Paddock
Kevin Plottner
MaryEllen Podgorski
and Suzanne Gooding

Illustration
H.B. Lewis

**Instructional
Illustration**
Sara Boore

Cover Design
Jon Valk

Rabbits Out of Hats
Patty Morris

**Prestidigitation and
Procrastination**
John Cassidy

**Prime Technical
Consultant**
Martin Gardner

Help from
T.A. Waters
Bob McAlister
Jeff Busby